Table of Contents

A Tasty Treat 4

The First Ice Cream 6

Ice Cream Inventors 10

From Farm to Factory 16

Cool Ice Cream Facts 24

    Make Your Own
       Ice Cream Sandwiches 28

    Glossary 30

    Read More 31

    Internet Sites 31

    Index 32

    About the Author 32

Words in **bold** appear in the glossary.

A Tasty Treat

Ring! Ring! Here comes the ice cream truck. People line up to buy a sweet treat. Everyone has a favorite flavor. What's yours?

Someone is celebrating a birthday. Guests share a giant sundae. There are so many scoops of ice cream topped with whipped cream! Yum!

Whether it comes in a cone, a bar, a sundae, a sandwich, or a shake, lots of people love ice cream. So where did it come from?

The First Ice Cream

Ice cream has been around for thousands of years. Long ago, people in Persia ate sweet ice water. They put fruit on top. In ancient China, people mixed snow, milk, and rice together.

More than 1,000 years later, an Italian explorer named Marco Polo traveled to China. Back home, he talked about the tasty treat. Cooks started to experiment. They added cream. This dessert was a bit like modern ice cream.

Marco Polo

King Charles I with his wife and two of their children

News of the dessert soon spread through Europe. An Italian duchess introduced ice cream to France. In England, King Charles I tried to keep it a secret. He paid his chef to stay quiet.

The king's plan didn't work. Ice cream made its way to the American **colonies** in the 1700s.

At first, ice cream was only for the rich. Later, people took ice from frozen lakes and ponds. They stored it in ice houses. This meant ice cream could be made all year.

Ice Cream Inventors

In 1718, Mary Eales published the first ice cream **recipe**. It called for cream inside a tin pot. Ice and salt were added around the outside of the pot. Salt made the cream freeze faster.

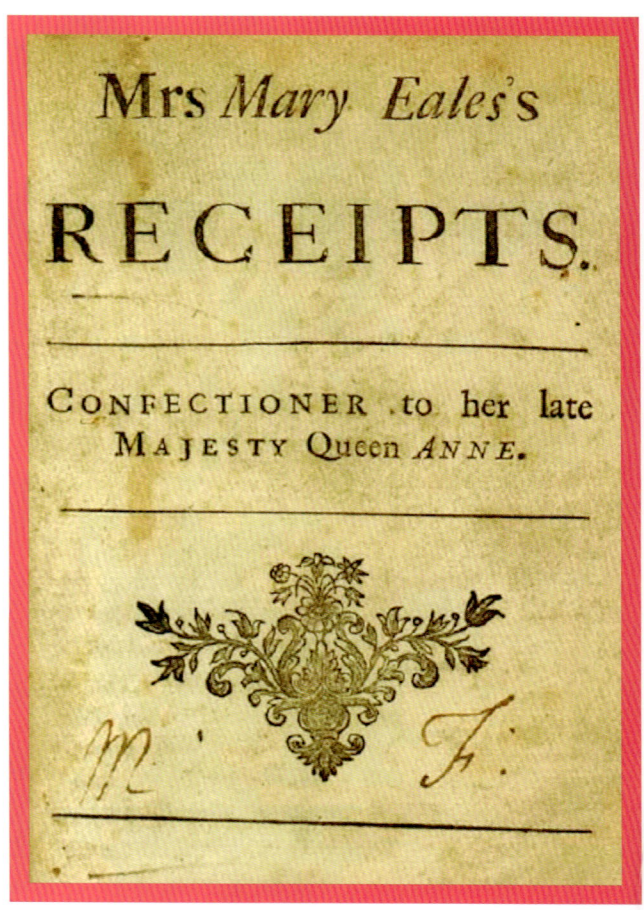

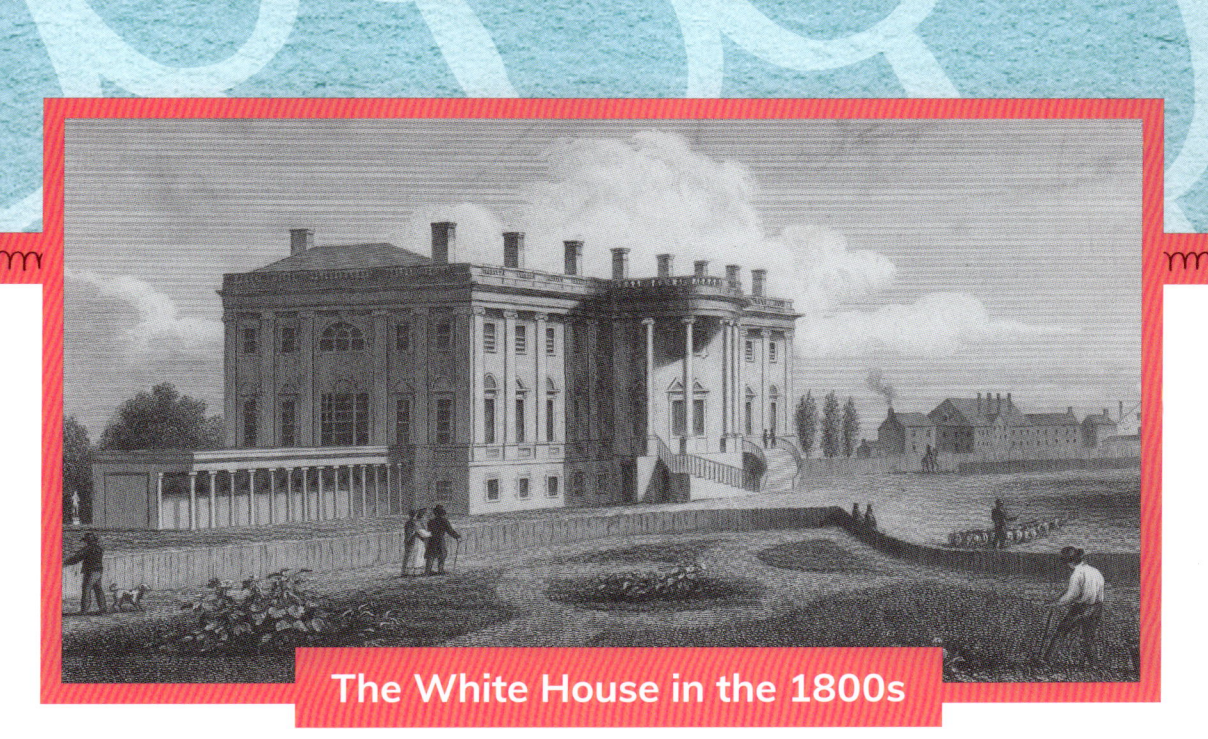

The White House in the 1800s

In the 1820s, a **White House** chef had the same idea. Augustus Jackson used ice and salt to get his ice cream cold and thick. He also added some salt into his creamy mixture. This made the popular dessert even more delicious!

Nancy Johnson invented the ice cream maker in 1843. She filled a wooden tub with ice and salt. Then she placed a smaller tub inside. A blade turned the liquid and added air. This made the ice cream soft.

An old-fashioned ice cream maker

Jacob Fussell

Jacob Fussell opened the first ice cream factory in 1851. He produced large amounts of ice cream. That meant more people could enjoy it! But grocery stores didn't start selling ice cream until the 1930s.

Who invented the ice cream cone? It was a man named Italo Marchiony. He first produced it in New York City in 1896. He received a **patent** for the idea in 1903.

A similar creation became popular at the 1904 **World's Fair**. An ice cream seller ran out of dishes. A nearby waffle seller had a solution. He rolled his waffles into cone shapes. They were then filled with ice cream.

A seller makes a waffle cone.

Good Humor ice cream trucks have been around since the 1920s.

In 1920, Harry Burt covered ice cream with a chocolate coating. He added a wooden stick. Later, he sold his Good Humor bars from trucks. Bells let people know it was time for ice cream.

From Farm to Factory

How is ice cream made today? It starts at dairy farms. Cows produce 6 to 8 gallons (23 to 30 liters) of milk each day. Some farmers use milking machines. **Suction cups** with tubes are attached to the cows' **udders**.

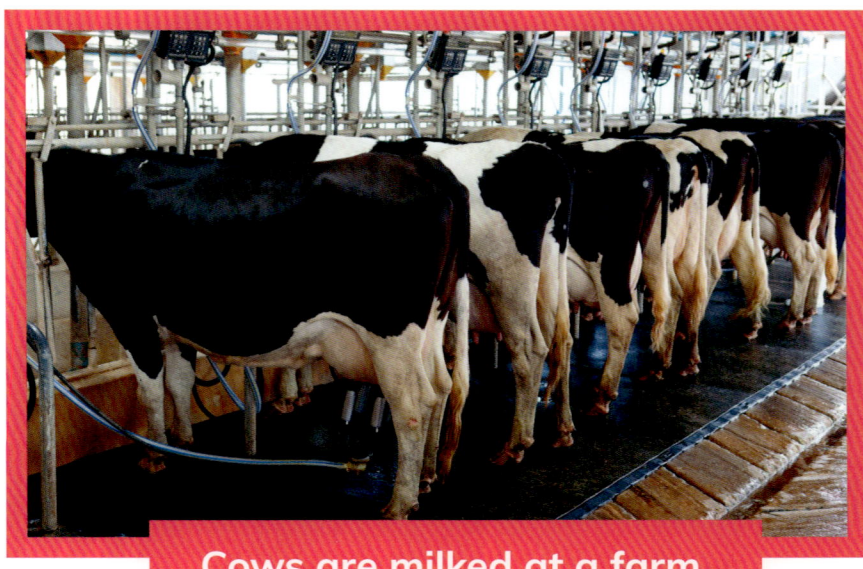

Cows are milked at a farm.

Milk travels through the tubes to a steel tank. The tank cools the milk. This keeps it fresh.

Next, a refrigerator truck comes to the farm. Milk is piped into the truck. Then it is on its way to a factory!

A refrigerator truck transports milk.

At the factory, milk is separated from cream. Milk goes into one cooling tank. Cream goes into the other. The tanks are kept cool at about 36 degrees Fahrenheit (2 degrees Celsius).

Then the milk and cream are combined. Cream makes ice cream smooth and thick. **Stabilizers** are also added. They keep the mixture from becoming icy. Sweeteners like sugar are added too.

Tanks in an ice cream factory

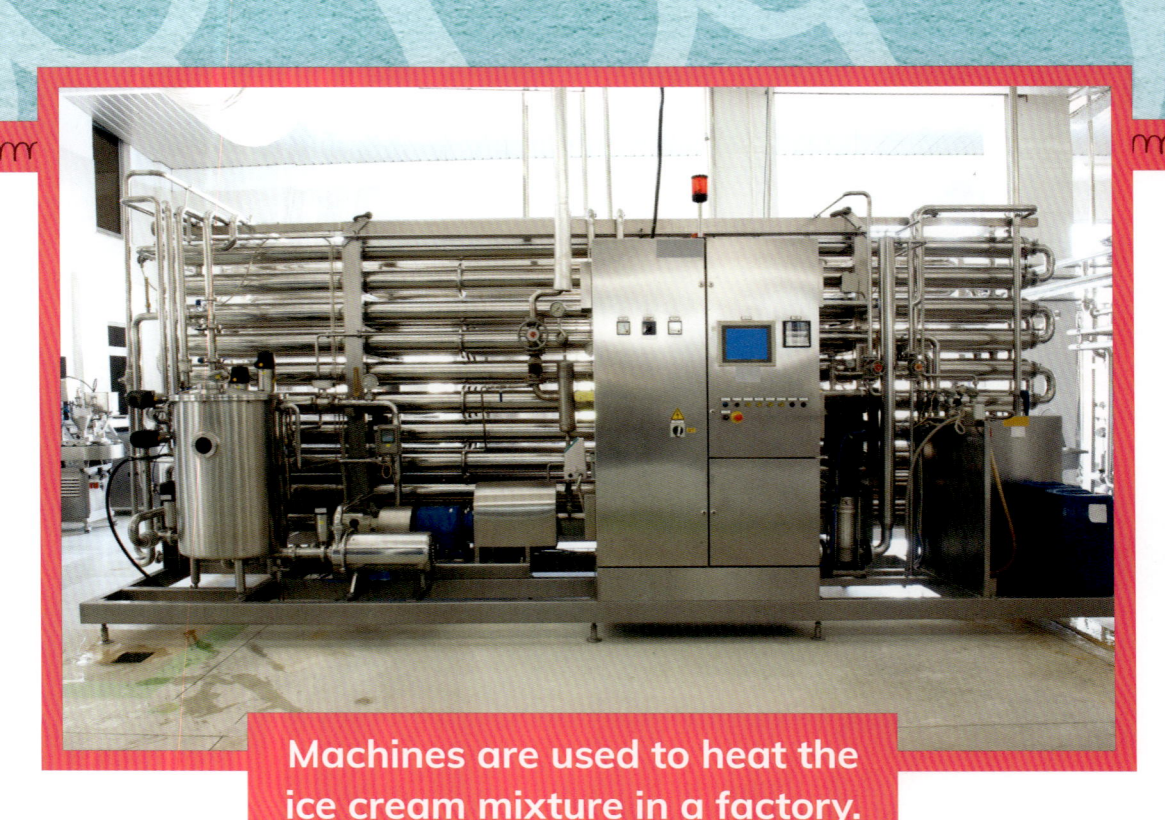

Machines are used to heat the ice cream mixture in a factory.

Next, the mixture is heated. This gets rid of harmful **bacteria**. Then the mixture is forced into a machine. The force breaks up bits of fat. The mixture cools for at least four hours.

Before the mixture freezes, flavors are added. There are so many choices! Factories make vanilla, chocolate, strawberry, mint chip, and more.

Each flavor is pumped into a mixing freezer. Blades stir the mixture and add air. This keeps ice cream soft.

Flavors are added to the ice cream mixture.

A carton of ice cream moves down a conveyor belt.

Each flavor of ice cream needs its own carton. The cartons move along a **conveyor belt**. A machine fills them.

Cartons move to a very cold room. The ice cream hardens. Then the cartons are covered in plastic. Finally, it is time for the ice cream to leave the factory!

Refrigerator trucks make deliveries to stores and restaurants. Ice cream parlors get giant tubs. There are so many places to buy and enjoy your favorite flavors!

Cool Ice Cream Facts

There are more than 1,000 different flavors of ice cream in the world. Vanilla is still the most popular.

In the United States, more ice cream is sold on Sunday than any other day of the week. In fact, the word *sundae* used to be spelled *sunday*!

The average American eats about 20 pounds (9 kilograms) of ice cream each year. That's more than anywhere else. The U.S also has National Ice Cream Month. It is celebrated in July.

There are many flavors of gelato.

There are also different versions of ice cream. Frozen yogurt is a healthier option. Gelato is like ice cream. It has more milk and less fat.

Halva is a candy made of sesame seeds. This flavor of ice cream is popular in Israel. In Turkey, people make dondurma. This treat pulls like taffy and doesn't melt as quickly as other ice cream.

Some people do not eat dairy. Instead, they enjoy ice pops or **sorbet**. There are also frozen treats made without dairy.

Sorbet is a dairy-free dessert.

Make Your Own Ice Cream Sandwiches

Head to the kitchen with a grown-up and some friends to make this yummy treat!

What You Need:

- baking sheet
- parchment paper or wax paper
- 1 package of your favorite cookies*
- 1 pint of ice cream, slightly softened
- ice cream scoop or paddle
- butter knife
- toppings: chocolate chips, nuts, or sprinkles
- plastic storage container with lid

*Choose cookies that are firm and not crumbly.

What You Do:

1. Line a baking sheet with parchment or wax paper.

2. Place cookies upside down on the baking sheet.

3. Place one scoop of ice cream onto each cookie and cover with another cookie. Gently press the cookies together to make a sandwich.

4. Smooth the edges of the sandwich with a butter knife.

5. Roll each sandwich in your favorite topping and return it to the baking sheet.

6. Put the baking sheet in the freezer for several hours until firm.

7. Store your ice cream sandwiches in the freezer in a plastic container with a lid. You can stack them, but make sure to separate the layers using parchment or wax paper.

Glossary

bacteria (bak-TEER-ee-uh)—very small living things that exist everywhere in nature

colony (KAH-luh-nee)—an area that has been settled by people from another country; a colony is ruled by another country

conveyor belt (kuhn-VAY-uhr BELT)—a belt moved by pulleys that carries items from one area to another

patent (PAT-uhnt)—a legal document giving someone sole rights to make or sell a product

recipe (RESS-i-pee)—directions for making and cooking food

sorbet (sawr-BEY)—a fruit-flavored ice served especially as dessert

stabilizer (STEY-buh-lahy-zer)—a substance added to another substance to prevent a change

suction cup (SUHK-shuhn CUHP)—a thin, rubbery cup that sticks to things

udder (UHD-uhr)—a baglike pouch on a cow's body that produces milk

White House (WAHYT HOUS)—the residence of the president of the United States

World's Fair (WURLDZ FAIR)—an exposition featuring exhibits and participants from around the world

Read More

Armand, Glenda and Kim Freeman. *Ice Cream Man: How Augustus Jackson Made a Sweet Treat Better.* New York: Crown Books for Young Readers, 2023.

Herrington, Lisa. *Desserts Around the World.* New York: Children's Press, 2022.

Knutson, Julie. *The Scoop on Ice Cream.* Ann Arbor, MI: Cherry Lake Publishing, 2022.

Internet Sites

Britannica Kids: Ice Cream
kids.britannica.com/students/article/ice-cream/275028

Kiddle: Ice Cream Facts for Kids
kids.kiddle.co/Ice_cream

Kidskonnect: Ice Cream Facts & Worksheets
kidskonnect.com/fun/ice-cream

Index

consumption, 25
dairy farms, 16
factories, 13, 16, 17, 18, 19, 20–21, 22–23
flavors, 4, 21, 22–23, 24, 26
frozen yogurt, 26
gelato, 26
Good Humor, 15
grocery stores, 13
ice cream cones, 5, 14
ice cream makers, 12
ice cream trucks, 4, 15
ice houses, 9
inventors
  Eales, Mary, 10
  Fussell, Jacob, 13
  Jackson, Augustus, 11
  Johnson, Nancy, 12
  Marchiony, Italo, 14
  Polo, Marco, 7
King Charles I, 8–9
National Ice Cream Month, 25
refrigerator trucks, 17, 23
salt, 10, 11, 12
sorbet, 27
sundaes, 5, 24
White House, 11
World's Fair, 14

About the Author

A public and a school librarian, Gloria Koster belongs to the Children's Book Committee of Bank Street College of Education. She enjoys both city and country life, dividing her time between Manhattan and the small town of Pound Ridge, New York. Gloria has three adult children and a bunch of energetic grandkids.